Copyright

© Uzochukwu Mike 2015

DEDICATION

This book is dedicated to unemployed young men and women across the globe who are making efforts to have better skills to achieve their dreams.

ACKNOWLEDGEMENTS

First, I acknowledge my parents who were able to train me to the university level. This made me get more exposed about life and adequate communication with people. Without sending me to school from the basic level to tertiary institution, I don't think you will be able to find this book on the internet. To be able to read and write is a big plus to life.

To my friend, late Igili Onyedika, I sincerely appreciate you. You made me know more about the internet and the opportunities it offers. You are a light to my life. I know you are with God almighty as you were a good person driven by love to help many youths live better lives through skill acquisition.

*This book is part of the book **"Basic Information in Youth and Youth Empowerment"**

CONTENTS

Chapter 1

Youth Unemployment

Unemployment is defined as the state of being without a paid job (Oxford Advanced Learners Dictionary, Fifth Edition). Unemployment occurs when people are without job and actively seeking for job (ILO 2013). It is a global issue as developed, developing, undeveloped and underdeveloped nations of the world are experiencing it. As evidence that even developed nations of the world are "combating" with unemployment, in December 2013, an estimate of 6.7 per cent Americans were unemployed. In the recent information from Ludwig Institute for Shared Economic Prosperity (LISEP), the headline unemployment rate in the United States of America was 4.2% for the month of May 2025. This statistic shows that many people in the country are still finding it difficult to earn money in the country including young people.

In 2012, International Labour Organization, one of the organizations that take statistics of both the employed and unemployed in the world, stated that about 6% of the world population is unemployed and that the most unemployed are the youths. International Labour Organization (ILO) also gives update on information that share boundary with labour in the general sense.

The most affected by unemployment are the youths. The number of jobless people around the world rose by 4 million in 2012 to 197 million. Young people were the worst affected: nearly 13% of those under 24 were unemployed. Some 35% of all young unemployed people have been out of work for six months or longer in advanced economies, up from 28.5% in 2007 (The Guardian 2013).

The global youth unemployment rate, estimated at 12.6 per cent in 2013, is close to its crisis peak. As many as 73 million young people are estimated to be unemployed in 2013. At the same time, informal employment among young people remains pervasive and transitions to decent work are slow and difficult (Global Employment Trends for Youth 2013).

Some Detailed Statistics on Youth Unemployment

Notable and reliable organizations all over the world have kept records of unemployment issues all over the world. International Labour Organization published record of unemployment statistics of the youths for interval of years.

Table 3.1: Global Unemployment rate of Youths (15 to 24 years) from 2007-13

	2007	2008	2009	2010	2011	2012p	2013p
Youth unemployment (millions)	69.9	70.4	75.6	74.0	72.6	72.9	73.4

Sourced from Trends Econometric Models, April 2013

It is important to note that from Table 3.1.

- 2012p are preliminary estimates; and
- 2013p–2018p are projections

There is high unemployment rate among graduates from secondary and tertiary institutions in the world. Many youths initially got admission into tertiary institutions of their choices with the hope of securing jobs after their graduation but in the world of today, it does not work out the way planned. Many youths graduated with their first degree from universities and could not secure good jobs. This made them to enrol into further studies in master's degree, but some at the end of their completion could not secure their dream jobs.

Table 3.2 Unemployment rate of youth with tertiary education, both sexes, 2000–11 (%)

Country	2000	2001	2002	2003	2004	2005	2006	2007	2008	2009	2010	2011	Change 2010-11
Austria	2.4	1.8	5.4	2.4	4.8	7.6	9.8	10.3	2.9	9.6	9.7	7.6	-2.1
Belgium	6.5	9.7	8.2	6.2	10.0	16.0	16.1	11.5	11.3	16.6	13.1	12.1	-1.0
Bulgaria	17.1	26.9	22.1	17.8	22.9	14.6	11.0	9.2	9.9	4.8	11.7	19.6	7.9
Cyprus	5.6	8.3	8.1	12.9	8.0	13.7	13.2	10.8	9.6	16.7	18.3	26.4	8.1
Czech Republic	13.7	15.1	8.8	13.5	9.5	16.1	14.1	9.2	8.1	13.3	15.0	12.3	-2.7
Denmark	1.0	10.0	11.8	7.3	17.6	5.4	10.8	5.7	4.8	7.1	15.6	14.6	-1.0
Estonia	16.7	26.2	2.8	3.7	25.8	7.6	5.8	4.5	8.1	8.7	17.8	15.2	-2.6
Finland	14.8	14.1	7.8	10.7	15.9	6.2	7.7	9.9	5.5	7.9	7.3	7.4	0.1
France	11.4	8.2	11.6	13.9	12.4	15.3	15.0	12.5	10.3	12.6	13.8	13.4	-0.4
Germany	6.8	3.8	4.9	5.4	7.1	12.0	9.0	6.5	7.0	6.0	6.6	4.5	-2.1
Greece	29.6	29.4	23.1	28.4	30.5	33.1	30.1	32.0	24.6	31.0	43.0	48.6	5.6
Hungary	4.8	4.3	6.2	6.0	10.3	12.9	16.7	12.1	15.0	18.5	22.2	19.7	-2.5
Ireland	2.7	2.7	4.9	4.7	4.3	6.4	5.4	5.6	7.5	17.0	18.8	17.8	-1.0
Italy	25.8	28.7	35.8	15.3	32.9	31.3	24.7	19.4	23.8	29.5	23.1	27.1	4.0
Latvia	6.5	7.2	13.6	13.4	7.6	5.3	6.0	4.2	7.9	22.2	20.4	14.6	-5.8
Lithuania	21.2	21.2	18.4	14.3	18.4	9.4	7.8	6.3	11.4	15.8	26.1	21.4	-4.7
Luxembourg	5.6	6.7	0.0	11.1	23.5	17.6	7.7	15.4	7.1	18.8	18.8	10.5	-8.3
Netherlands	2.4	4.9	1.8	4.8	3.5	4.8	2.6	2.6	2.9	4.5	5.2	4.4	-0.8
Norway	8.2	9.5	8.6	8.6	11.7	7.2	5.1	2.9	3.6	4.8	5.5	5.4	-0.1
Poland	26.1	29.0	27.5	27.7	31.0	29.3	23.2	20.0	16.8	19.6	20.7	22.0	1.3
Portugal	6.9	9.7	13.4	14.6	13.2	24.3	28.8	26.1	27.2	24.4	26.2	29.0	2.8
Romania	9.2	17.2	19.7	15.7	13.1	22.0	27.6	21.1	20.4	24.8	28.9	29.3	0.4
Slovakia	26.9	24.1	21.4	23.4	24.4	17.2	16.3	18.9	15.5	22.4	27.3	24.0	-3.3
Slovenia	6.3	7.1	25.0	8.0	12.1	18.4	17.1	8.8	17.8	12.5	16.7	18.2	1.5
Spain	26.6	20.0	21.6	19.6	22.1	17.1	15.1	13.6	15.9	26.0	28.9	35.0	6.1
Sweden	2.4	3.4	7.4	5.2	11.7	16.0	12.8	12.2	11.5	12.8	14.7	12.4	-2.3
Switzerland	4.4	19.2	7.3	11.6	2.3	11.2	13.5	6.7	8.1	6.3	7.2	8.5	1.3
United Kingdom	5.6	5.1	5.9	5.3	4.1	7.9	9.1	7.5	9.2	13.0	12.1	12.0	-0.1

Source: Eurostat online database.

In table 3.2, it shows that acquiring certificates as a graduate from universities, polytechnics, or even colleges do not guarantee any of having a job. Taking Greece as a case study, in the year 2011, the data sourced from Eurostat show that 48.6% tertiary institution graduates of the country were unemployed.

In African countries, the average record of unemployed tertiary institution graduates is higher than that found in Europe and other developed countries in the world. In Nigeria for instance, the statistics of unemployed Nigerian graduates which are mainly youths is outrageous. According to Thisday News (a news publication company in Nigeria) on 15th November 2012, about 60% of Nigerian graduates are unemployed.

Another study on the statistics of the unemployed youths with secondary education in some countries shows the there is also the issue of unemployment among these youths. This is explained in detail in Table 3.3.

Table 3.3: Unemployment rate of youth with secondary education, both sexes, 2000–11 (%)

Country	2000	2001	2002	2003	2004	2005	2006	2007	2008	2009	2010	2011	Change 2010–11
Austria	5.4	4.9	6.6	6.3	8.1	8.0	6.5	6.2	5.7	7.5	7.0	6.2	-0.8
Belgium	14.4	9.7	13.3	18.3	17.2	19.7	18.0	17.5	16.2	20.5	19.9	15.5	-4.4
Bulgaria	30.4	33.3	31.0	23.1	19.7	17.5	15.3	12.3	9.6	14.1	21.2	23.6	2.4
Cyprus	11.3	7.6	5.9	5.4	6.0	13.9	8.9	9.0	8.3	13.7	17.4	23.0	5.6
Czech Republic	14.1	13.2	13.0	13.9	16.7	16.4	14.9	8.6	7.1	13.7	15.7	15.2	-0.5
Denmark	7.5	7.6	5.4	6.6	7.7	8.0	6.3	5.7	6.2	10.3	11.5	11.5	0.0
Estonia	17.4	21.8	12.4	23.4	18.5	16.2	10.7	7.2	10.3	24.9	31.3	21.0	-10.3
Finland	20.5	19.4	18.9	19.7	18.9	16.1	14.1	11.8	11.2	16.8	16.9	14.9	-2.0
France	17.7	15.1	16.1	14.7	17.7	17.9	18.6	16.1	16.8	21.0	20.1	19.4	-0.7
Germany	7.0	7.1	8.9	10.5	13.4	13.6	11.1	8.8	8.1	9.2	7.4	6.0	-1.4
Greece	31.8	30.1	28.7	28.0	27.4	27.6	26.1	23.7	23.2	26.6	31.4	43.8	12.4
Hungary	11.0	9.4	10.0	10.5	12.0	17.1	15.7	15.6	16.9	22.5	23.3	23.0	-0.3
Ireland	4.2	4.9	6.4	6.9	6.3	6.5	7.3	7.3	11.2	23.0	26.3	27.9	1.6
Italy	31.7	27.1	25.8	25.5	21.3	22.0	19.9	19.0	19.9	24.1	26.5	27.3	0.8
Latvia	17.8	19.1	21.1	14.6	18.4	10.1	8.8	9.4	11.1	29.1	33.2	32.0	-1.2
Lithuania	26.1	30.5	18.3	26.8	23.0	17.4	9.8	8.2	11.1	29.0	33.9	33.3	-0.6
Luxembourg	4.8	4.8	4.2	9.4	12.7	9.1	11.1	9.0	15.0	13.2	9.7	12.3	2.6
Netherlands	2.8	2.3	2.8	4.5	5.6	5.7	4.2	3.9	3.5	4.6	6.4	5.3	-1.1
Norway	7.0	7.8	7.6	8.9	11.3	8.8	6.1	4.6	4.2	6.2	6.3	5.9	-0.4
Poland	35.7	39.9	42.2	42.9	40.6	37.0	29.5	21.7	16.9	20.2	23.1	25.4	2.3
Portugal	8.4	9.8	9.6	12.9	11.2	15.3	16.0	14.8	14.4	18.2	21.3	27.3	6.0
Romania	22.0	21.0	25.0	22.8	24.0	22.5	22.0	21.0	17.5	20.9	24.6	25.4	0.8
Slovakia	35.0	36.7	35.6	30.6	28.6	25.1	21.4	15.3	14.6	24.3	30.6	30.7	0.1
Slovenia	14.5	13.5	12.4	13.8	13.1	14.8	12.9	9.4	10.1	12.3	12.9	15.4	0.5
Spain	25.7	21.5	21.5	22.0	21.0	17.2	16.1	16.6	19.6	31.1	34.3	41.5	7.2
Sweden	9.4	7.1	8.4	10.1	13.6	16.0	14.5	12.1	11.8	18.4	18.7	18.0	-0.7
Switzerland	5.4	3.3	5.5	8.5	7.0	7.7	7.9	6.5	7.1	9.1	8.1	7.5	-0.6
United Kingdom	8.6	7.2	7.5	8.2	7.7	9.5	10.7	11.0	11.2	15.6	16.8	18.9	2.1

Source: Eurostat online database.

In Table 3.3, Poland, Greece, Italy, and Spain have high youth unemployment rate of those who completed their secondary school educations. From the data sourced from Eurostat, in the year 2003, 42.9% of secondary school graduates in Poland were unemployed. This is challenging and the youths are not happy at all with such which make them to be in bad mood. It is a nightmare to them.

Greece on the other hand is battling with unemployment in Europe. From the statistics, in the year 2011, 43.8% of youths who are Greece citizens and attended secondary school were unemployed. Those who are affected with the menace are having sleepless nights as they are confused and frustrated. Many are praying day in and out for God's intervention on the situation.

In the interval of years given in the record, Italy has highest unemployed secondary school graduates in the year 2000. In that year, 31.7% of the secondary school graduates were unemployed. The decrease in the unemployment rate among the category is not constant. It decreases within intervals and at a point increases.

Spain is another European country with high secondary school graduates based on the record. Though many who are not citizens of Spain are working hard to immigrate to the country, there is evidence of unemployment in the country. Both government and citizens of the country are working to ensure that unemployment in the country is reduced.

Table 3.4: Share of unemployed youth who have been unemployed for at least six months, both sexes, 2000–11 (%)

Country	2000	2001	2002	2003	2004	2005	2006	2007	2008	2009	2010	2011
Australia	32.2	29.8	27.3	25.6	24.8	22.4	23.6	21.3	20.0	23.4	26.4	26.2
Austria	26.7	27.5	17.5	28.1	36.2	30.9	33.2	32.3	29.2	30.8	35.0	31.6
Belgium	54.2	55.0	47.4	46.8	45.3	46.3	45.9	48.2	42.9	45.3	52.7	48.3
Canada	8.5	7.1	7.2	7.4	7.0	7.0	5.7	5.0	5.2	8.1	9.8	10.2
Czech Republic	60.8	60.4	56.6	56.4	59.7	60.4	61.7	53.7	52.1	43.7	53.0	53.2
Denmark	6.1	12.8	14.4	20.2	15.2	12.3	13.2	11.0	8.2	12.6	18.4	24.6
Estonia	41.6	48.2	46.5	48.8	51.9	43.6	34.2	38.8	37.1	47.5	60.5	54.2
Finland	19.1	16.0	16.5	15.7	16.2	15.8	13.8	15.8	9.6	13.7	16.8	12.9
France	42.3	42.1	39.2	43.5	41.9	43.5	45.0	43.0	41.2	46.7	48.2	47.1
Germany	48.0	45.0	47.6	50.8	50.2	52.4	52.3	51.0	47.0	46.2	45.1	41.7
Greece	71.0	64.8	67.3	68.0	68.5	64.7	69.0	62.2	57.5	50.7	55.1	60.6
Hungary	61.0	56.2	57.1	55.5	57.6	59.2	59.8	59.8	55.6	57.4	65.9	59.1
Iceland	-	9.6	20.2	7.5	6.9	3.4	3.9	-	3.2	14.2	27.8	20.6
Ireland	-	38.4	37.5	40.0	42.0	38.4	39.2	36.3	36.6	48.7	60.6	63.8
Israel	18.6	17.4	20.3	25.1	26.9	25.7	26.7	24.3	21.9	23.2	22.9	18.1
Italy	78.7	78.5	73.2	72.9	56.8	59.7	58.3	54.7	52.9	58.1	61.1	63.2
Japan	40.0	34.9	40.3	40.9	44.8	41.8	38.8	37.8	35.7	39.2	49.0	50.0
Korea, Republic of	8.9	8.8	9.2	5.9	8.3	8.7	9.0	8.8	8.1	5.1	-	3.4
Luxembourg	24.2	29.1	33.8	23.7	38.6	32.1	47.9	39.2	46.3	36.3	39.1	42.7
Mexico	3.9	3.0	3.8	3.3	3.0	5.7	4.2	3.4	2.9	4.1	4.2	3.3
Netherlands	-	-	20.7	30.2	34.5	38.5	37.1	31.3	25.3	26.3	28.8	28.7
New Zealand	24.7	20.2	16.2	18.0	15.6	11.8	14.0	11.2	10.0	16.4	20.1	21.1
Norway	6.7	4.5	7.8	9.1	7.7	8.6	13.9	12.7	7.2	11.7	17.0	17.8
Poland	53.7	58.3	62.8	61.2	58.6	59.9	56.2	49.1	34.4	33.5	36.3	42.7
Portugal	41.9	42.2	40.7	43.7	49.3	52.2	48.7	46.3	43.3	48.2	50.8	46.0
Slovakia	66.9	67.6	70.5	68.1	68.5	73.9	72.5	68.2	65.8	57.8	70.0	70.7
Slovenia	-	-	63.4	60.6	59.7	55.2	56.1	46.7	37.0	40.5	50.7	52.6
Spain	53.9	49.3	43.4	45.2	42.8	28.2	24.2	23.7	25.5	41.2	49.8	53.2
Sweden	18.2	16.1	18.6	17.8	20.0	-	-	12.2	11.2	15.0	19.0	15.8
Turkey	35.0	34.8	43.0	38.5	56.2	53.4	49.3	44.2	40.1	41.6	40.9	37.3
United Kingdom	30.2	30.0	24.4	24.3	26.7	27.9	30.5	31.1	31.5	38.9	43.5	43.9
United States	7.3	8.2	11.3	13.6	14.2	12.9	11.9	12.0	13.9	23.3	29.7	30.1
Russian Federation	53.2	45.4	45.9	44.4	45.9	45.1	47.5	47.6	38.3	36.9	36.0	40.4
OECD countries	34.6	32.6	32.9	32.9	33.3	32.9	31.5	28.5	26.0	31.1	35.2	35.3
OECD Europe	50.4	49.3	48.3	47.6	48.1	47.3	45.7	41.4	37.5	41.8	45.2	45.6

- = not available.
Source: OECD online database.

Another standard through which international bodies use in accessing unemployment among people in the world is by six months interval. The percentage given is higher when compared with the unemployed youths in Table 3.1, 3.2, and 3.3.

Luxembourg which is the world second richest country in 2013 notwithstanding their riches still combats with youth unemployment. The report is according to International Monetary Fund World Economic Outlook Database, April 2013, and they took after Qatar which is the world richest country. Looking at Table 3.4, Luxembourg has the high number of unemployed youths for interval of six months in the year 2006. This accounts for 47.9% of the youths' population.

Italy is another country which has been visited by youth unemployment in a very highway based on the report from Table 3.4. The number of the unemployed youth for the period of six months is one of the highest in the report. In 2000, 2001, and 2002, statistics has it that a total 78.7%, 78.5%, and 73.2% Italian youths were respectively unemployed for six good months.

Slovakia is another country that is still suffering under the visit that unemployment paid to them. The country ranks high among the countries with youth unemployment for a period of six months. In 2005 and 2006, 73.9 and 72.5% of the country's youths were respectively unemployed for a period of six months.

Chapter 2

Causes of Youth Unemployment

In this chapter, we will focus on the causes of youth unemployment across many countries. Understanding these causes will go a long way in helping both individuals and government discover approach to reduce it to the minimal level. It is one important factor to consider before the arrest of this issue that is making our young people unhappy.

The whole causes of youth unemployment in the world cannot be detailed out in this book, but some of the causes are to be explained. Some authors may have the causes of youth unemployment among nations as like the one to be listed and explained while others may have something that is slightly different to those ones to be explained. Hence, the causes of youth unemployment are as follow:

- Corruption.
- Bad government.
- Laziness.
- Inadequate skills
- Improper funding of Institutions
- Poor savings
- Poor planning
- Poor implementation of youth empowerment programmes/schemes

- Pride
- Selfishness
- Economic recession; and
- Poverty/low investment.

The above points listed as the causes of youth unemployment in the world are to be discussed sub-heading by sub-heading for more understanding and clarity.

How Corruption Contributes to Youth Unemployment

Corruption is dishonest or fraudulent conduct by those in power, typically involving bribery. It is criminal act that have contributed a lot to youth unemployment in the present world. Corruption among ministers and presidents of various countries has retarded the growth and development of the world youths. Corruption is illegitimate use of power to benefit a private interest (Morris 1991). Corruption is one of the major causes of youth unemployment in many ways. When a corrupt government that suppose to build industries for youths to get employed is busy embezzling the money for his selfish interest, what do you think will happen to the youth unemployment status? The youth unemployment will be of high increase because the fund that supposed to be used for creation of jobs is being taken and embezzled by group of persons that called themselves government.

Report has shown that presidents of nations with low transparency according to the judgement of Transparency International Perception have smuggled out huge amount of money from their countries into foreign banks. When this kind of thing occurs, the youths become the one to suffer as the money that will be used in development of their countries is hidden in another man's country. According to clerk Gascoigne, spokesperson for GFI, the organization's latest available research data show that the amount of money that Ethiopia lost to smuggling of cash out of the country, both by the government and private sector between 2001 and 2010, totals 16.5 billion U.S dollars (Tadias Magazine 2013). Yet, the Ethiopian youths are perishing in unemployment.

From the above report, it shows that Ethiopians that indulged in the dirty game were busy promoting the economy of other countries while allowing the youths and the entire citizens to suffer unemployment. When the government and other private sector quietly smuggle such amount out, how much is left for training and equipping the youths to minimize unemployment among them?

Bad Governance and Youth Unemployment

A bad government can be a cause of youth unemployment in any society. A government that lacks leadership skill cannot even secure employment for the adult citizens in a country not to talk of providing employment for the youth of her country. The problems that many nations are having today are because of bad governments that do not know their left to their right.

The reason for the bad leadership could be because of godfatherism. Godfathers are generally defined as men who have the power personally to determine both who gets nominated to contest elections and who wins in the election (Gross Archive 2014). Some political leaders before they enter into leadership usually have godfathers. The godfathers that put them into leadership positions usually demand for ransom from them as agreement before occupying the sits. The demand may be too much that the money the government would have been used for development of the youths and creation of unemployment is given to one retired and tired human being in the name of godfather.

In Nigeria, Liberia, Ethiopia, Sierra Leone, India, French, Mexico, and some other countries, there is evidence of godfatherism that have existed. It has become almost impossible for an individual to hold political office either by appointment or election without patronizing a godfather because of their power and influence (Gross Archive 2014). These godfathers in many countries often control the actions of those in leadership. The one that leads may have the interest to do all he could do to curb youth unemployment while the godfather will be interested to take large proportion of the money for his personal and selfish interest.

Some governments do not have the ability to organise. Ability to organise is one of the characteristics of good leadership. A leader who cannot organize properly is likely to cause youth unemployment. When he organises, he has the possibility of looking into the affairs of the youths and solve unemployment issue. Again, governments that cannot organise can spend the country's fund extravagantly and then result to failure in creation of employment for the citizens.

Laziness

To be lazy is to be unwilling to work or use energy. Laziness is the inability of a person to think critically, find out possible solutions to challenges, and then not propelled to work using his or her energy to make changes. Laziness is disease that many youths have been suffering from for years now. It has infected many and is eating down to their bone marrows.

Many youths have received their walking papers from offices because of laziness (sacked). The management would have been warning them for their unwillingness to work before such bad incidence occurred. Some claimed that they cannot work for a particular management till their death but all centres on laziness.

Some youths are lazy to work but are not tired in having premarital sex. They do this most often before going to work; yet they are not married. Because of the "hard work" they usually perform with the opposite sex before they go to work in their employed places, they become dizzy and lazy to work when the management assign duties to them. Some of them during weekend cannot allow what is in-between their legs to rest for once. They keep moving from one brothel to another, one party to another which make them to be weakened and lazy on the workdays.

Even though there is no secured and assured established companies or offices that can employed the youths in some parts of the world, some youths are not willing to work on their own to create jobs for themselves. Many of them believe they cannot create self-employed jobs for themselves, and that is a sign of laziness found in most youths.

Hard labour does not kill in anyway. Youths who engage in hard labour to make their money in the first place cannot in any way squander the money without making good use of them. Some youths are too lazy to take part in hard work, create wealth for themselves and then finally invest in other businesses of their choice to make better and higher money in future.

Inadequate skills and Youth Unemployment

Inadequate skill is one of the major causes of youth unemployment in the entire universe. What can a youth who has not skill offer to any organization when he or she gets employed in any company? What will an establishment do with an individual that has acquired no skill on the area of the work he wants to get employed? Inadequate skills have kept many youths in the state of unemployment for many years; yet some are still sitting in their parents' homes without having any second thought on how they can acquire skill and help themselves in such situation.

A non-skilful youth is more of like a liability to any company. The reason is because he cannot add much to the growth of an organization. Going for skills by the world youths will be an added advantage to solving youth unemployment in the world. Companies look for skilful job seekers as they know such people will add good values to the growth of their establishments.

The unemployment among youths who are university and college graduates is because skill acquisition is lacking in them. Some tertiary education sectors are filled with theories without good practical backup. This makes large number of graduates from universities to be unemployed.

In the field of engineering, there are many graduates from the field that cannot boast of being engineers because their kind of engineers is that of pen and paper. Installing of some machines that will impact skills on those that study engineering in high schools will limit the high rate of unemployment in many nations. The importance of skill acquisition should not be underrated in the field of engineering study and that will be promoted through installation of necessary machines.

Improper funding of Institutions

Who is funding of institutions made for? Do you think funding of institutions is made for the government alone or can individuals in a country get involved? Funding of institutions is made for both the government and the citizens of a country. It is not a must that the first son of a family must make all the necessary expenses in his father's funeral when the younger in the family is the richest. When a government fails, the rich individuals can sponsor.

Many institutions in some countries do receive the attention they need to give quality service and create employment opportunities for the masses. Because of this challenge, unemployment state has been of high increase. Selfish governments are embezzling public funds for their selfish interest without looking into the infrastructural standards of their countries.

In various colleges, the classrooms where students study are nothing to write home about. The windows have been eaten up by ants, the boards used for studies out of date, and the roof of their lecture halls destroyed. This makes the students that study in such institutions to be half baked and graduate with no standard backup.

Poor savings

Many youths are suffering from unemployment because of their inability to make good servings and from the savings create a better wealth in future. Some do not think well on what the future holds for them which will propel them into good money saving to invest into businesses.

Poor saving culture among the youth serves as a major setback for accessing credit for start-ups. Young people hoping to be entrepreneurs must be made to understand that commercial banks and lending institutions are there primarily to protect and add value to share holder's investment (Olajire and Comfort 2013).

When a youth knows and understand that there is high youth unemployment in the world and began to make savings on time, he can start something with the money he saved and make impact in the society when his wealth grows. Some youths cannot adopt saving culture. They believe in the principle "let's spend all today and think later of tomorrow when it comes". This habit has been adding to the high increase of the unemployed youths from year to year, which is really a sour taste.

Youths who were into tertiary institutions were making some money through relatives and friends that usually sent money to them as of those days. They squandered these money as if there was no tomorrow. Today, many of such persons are being caught by unemployment and what they continued saying is "had it been I knew".

Poor planning

Truly, failing to plan is planning to fail. Youths have fallen into the pit of unemployment because they did not plan on time. When youths do not plan on time on how their future is likely to be, they are prone to unemployment which is one of the major challenges they are facing today.

A youth who finished his study at the age of about 26 years and plan to marry at the age of 33 years, and build house at 40, will be propelled to convert good opportunities that come to him to jobs.

In the side of the governments of various countries, poor planning by them have resulted to massive youth unemployment. When governments make plans on how to create employment for the youths, the allocation to be given for women empowerment, the allocation for educational funding, that for road network construction, that for health department, and so on, all will be met smoothly. But for governments that do not make these plans with good ministers to carry out the functions effectively, disorderliness becomes what will be noticed, which contributes to youth unemployment.

Poor Implementation of Youth Empowerment Programmes/Schemes

Although there are many youth empowerment associations, organizations, and schemes, the problem is on their implementation. In their offices, you see lots of their workers, but do they meet the standard of the work they are called to do? Some of them come to offices just to go back to their residents without making much impact on the work they are called to do. They drive expensive cars, wear expensive clothes, live in expensive mansions, and attend night club parties, without doing the exact function they are supposed to do. In public places and occasions, they are called big names forgetting the fact that the youths which they are called to empower are suffering and wandering like sheep without a shepherd.

The government do not implement the laws guiding these organizations and that is why the workers are careless and incompetent. What the government owns is not properly cared for because the people believe that the government will not have time to monitor them. If the government do not implement these organizations or programmes by changing the weak and incompetent workers, the unemployment among youths will continue to be of increase. Paying no attention to these youth empowerment organizations is as good as having none of them in the country.

It is like a man who hides his money in a cupboard thinking that in the next ten years that the money will give birth to larger amount. On going back to the cupboard after ten years, he found out that rats has eaten all the paper money with only pieces left there. In this instance, the money would have yield more for the man if he invested it in booming business, but it happened that he lost at the end. This is what happens when government do not implement youth empowerment organizations. Instead of gaining from the empowered youths through the organizations, they continue to loss as they continue to pay organizations that perform none of the duties they are called to do for the good of the youths.

Pride

Oxford Advanced Learner's Dictionary defines pride as a feeling of deep pleasure or satisfaction derived from achievements, qualities, or possessions that do one credit. It further defined it as consciousness of one's own dignity; the quality of having an excessively high option for oneself. The joblessness among many youths is not only because of the failure from government but also from failure that comes from the youths themselves.

Some youths feel very high that they cannot start from little to accumulate big. They want to be as rich as Bill Gate overnight. They think that it is abnormal for them to pick small jobs because they are the big boys in the town. When they are given jobs that will fetch them small money at the start, they reject it thinking that one day they will hit big time job that will yield big time money for them. The Bill Gate that the world celebrates today started small and not as big as what people think.

Learned and educated agricultural scientists that are youths vowed that they must work in the field they specialized in without understanding that the world is dynamic. Because of this, they are included as the unemployed youths even when they are offered jobs which are not mainly in their area of specialization. Pride is one of the factors that have been contributing yearly on the youth unemployment rate.

Selfishness

Political leaders are so selfish that what they care for is what will benefit them and their family and nothing else. They embezzle the money that is supposed to be used for community development and use it alone for their own need. As a result of this attitude, youth unemployment continues to increase instead of decreasing.

The poorly funded universities in various part of the world can be because of the selfish interests of both the government leaders and that of the school heads. Many of these leaders sent their children to countries where their standard of education is unique thereby paying lips service to that in their country. They easily forget the fact that it is their fellow political leaders that are ruling in the foreign countries that make the university standard of their own countries what they are. It is because of selfish interest of many heads of departments that make them misuse the fund given to them to equip the universities and colleges in their countries so that the students will acquire important skills that will help them to be self-employed after their education.

Many youths have quitted from the work they were doing before in some managements because of selfish interests of the owners of such organizations. When they quit from jobs, their numbers become added to the number of unemployed youths in the universe. When the management they work on daily basis underpaid them, their next line of actions is on how to quit from such kind of job because the money paid to them cannot in any way help in solving their needs. It is not as if the management does not make enough which he will pay them with, but all centres of the selfishness of the proprietor. He wants the workers to be working, and he earns and used the money alone.

Another face of selfishness that causes youth unemployment is found in hiding of information. Information is power and the amount of good information received by a person determines how far the person will go. When youths are feed with the right information that will help them excel in the present world, there become possibilities of becoming rich, open more establishments, and employ the masses in their country and beyond.

The issue here is that some business managers and those that have the information that can help the youths to get employed do not want to let them out. They sometimes demand for huge amount of money from the youths which they cannot be able to pay before they get it. In the world of computer for instance, there are many lucrative skills that would have helped the youth secure important good-paying jobs, but those who have this kind of information do not want others to know about them. Such kinds of persons believe that they are the only persons that are to know it and become kings alone-just because of their own selfishness.

Youths suffer because of lack of knowledge. The knowledge would have been obtained through information which will help reduce youth unemployment, but those that have the information are holding them captive. When youths meet craftsmen to teach them skills on a particular field, these men sometimes release such information that will be helpful to them and in return create employment for them. The author of this book is witness to that because he has had such experience from a craftsman. They either demand some huge amount of money or tell tall story all because of their selfishness.

Economic Recession

Economic recession is another factor that has contributed greatly to youth unemployment in the world. This does not only affect the youths but the entire world in a very bad way. In economics, a recession is a business cycle contraction. It is a general slowdown in economic activity (Merriam-Webster Online Dictionary 2014). Macroeconomic indicators such as GDP (Gross Domestic Product), investment spending, capacity utilization, household income, business profits, and inflation fall, while bankruptcies and the unemployment rate rise (Wikipedia 2014).

When there is economic recession in any country, the country usually faces unemployment. There becomes less cash flow in the country's economy and the Gross Domestic Product (GDP) of the country reduces. What it implies is that at this point, both private and government investments decrease which leads to drop in employment rate of the country. Africa, Asia, Europe, North, and South American countries have in one way or the other witnessed economic recession which resulted to dismissing of workers that have been working in some organizations.

United States of America was hit by economic recession in 2007-2008. U.S. employers shed 63,000 jobs in February 2008 (Job Loss Predictions 2007), the most in five years. Former Federal Reserve chairman Alan Greenspan said on 6 April 2008 that "There is more than a 50 percent chance the United States could go into recession." According to a report from Bureau of Economic Analysis of United States, in September 2008, 156,000 jobs were lost in the country. As if that was not enough, the recession continued. In November of the same year (2008), employers eliminated 533,000 jobs, the largest single month loss in 34 years (Uchitelle, Andrews and Labaton 2008). The total number of jobs lost in United States in 2008 was estimated to be 2.6 million.

The experience that United States had is also witnessed in other states worldwide. When such joblessness occurs, it also affects the world youths which keeps unemployment among them rising.

Poverty/low investment

Poverty and low investment are among the causes of youth unemployment. A poor youth may have ideas that he will use to secure employment for his or herself but because there is no money to convert the idea to money, he or she remains unemployed. The ideas continue to rotten and decay because there is no money for establishment.

On the other hand, low investment by manufacturing companies and organizations is one of the causes of youth unemployment in various parts of the world. Think of a situation where more than one hundred thousand youth engineers graduate from universities on yearly basis and for a period of five years no engineering company has invested in the country. What do you think will be the condition of the young engineers? The truth remain that there will be serious unemployment rate among the youths of such country.

Countries that have poor investment from foreign companies could be dependent on several factors. These factors can include corruption, non-availability of the necessary resources, and fear of failure.

Corruption has been a major factor that has scared many companies away from good investors that would have increased the employment opportunities of citizens. When companies have interest in investing in that country, at a point, they might have a rethink that since there is high corruption in that country, the people may steal their working accessories or dupe them. Because of the challenge, the companies withdraw their interest from coming into such countries.

Another factor that leads to poor investment is non-availability of the required resources. Countries that do not have good natural resources to attract investors usually receive small number of foreign investors. A company that manufactures with limestone as their major raw material cannot invest in countries that do not have that. If they do otherwise, the possibility of succeeding will be small because they will spend much in sourcing the material from another country other than where they manufacture. Because of this, when the products are manufactured, they will be sold at higher price than what it would have been if the countries have the resources.

Conclusion

Youth unemployment is a big challenge that many nations are facing. This challenge pisses many people off and give others sleepless night. The facts and figures presented in this chapter 'Youth Unemployment' and the 'Causes of Youth Unemployment' in the world is no tall story. Once again, discussed in this chapter is youth unemployment, which includes statistics on youth unemployment and causes.

References

- Eurostat, Ireland Youth Unemployment Rate, retrieved March 6, 2015

- International Labour Organization (2013), Unemployment Report, retrieved September 24, 2015

- International Labour Organization (2013), World unemployment figures set to rise in 2013, claims UN labour agency

- International Labour Organization (2013), Global Employment Trends for Youth 2013: A generation at risk, Geneva, pp 10

- Morris, S.D. (1991), Corruption and Politics in Contemporary Mexico. University of Alabama Press, Tuscaloosa

- Olajire A.A and Comfort O.A. Entrepreneurship education and youth empowerment in contemporary Nigeria. Scholarly Journal of Education Vol. 2(5), pp. 52-57

- Wikipedia (2014), Recession, retrieved January 3, 2015

About the Author

Uzochukwu Mike, Peter, is a young author who has been making good impact in the field of book writing and publication. He is from Oba in Idemili South Local Government Area of Anambra state, Nigeria. He writes mainly educational books. He is also a website, application, and graphics designer, teacher and mentor to those who need guide in their life activities. He likes making impact in the lives of the world youths through his publications.

Academically, he holds bachelor's degree in metallurgical and Materials Engineering (B. Eng). He is an intelligent fellow and that made him began his writing career when he was still an undergraduate student in the university. Before his graduation from the university, he had already published more than three books which have been selling in Amazon.com.

He also has a blog where he publishes free articles that cut across education and topics that address challenges that nations are facing. His free articles have helped many people including the youths and adult.

Index

www.ingramcontent.com/pod-product-compliance
Lightning Source LLC
Chambersburg PA
CBHW061234180526
45170CB00003B/1290